The **Official**

Candy Crush SAGA

Top Tips Guide

sphere

SPHERE

First published in Great Britain in 2015 by Sphere

Copyright © Little, Brown Book Group 2015.

"King", "Candy Crush" and associated marks
and logos are trademarks of King.com Ltd
or related entities and are used under license
by Little, Brown Book Group.

1 3 5 7 9 10 8 6 4 2

A CIP catalogue record for this book
is available from the British Library.

ISBN 978-0-7515-6395-5

Printed and bound in Great Britain by
Clays Ltd, St Ives plc

Papers used by Sphere are from well-managed
forests and other responsible sources.

MIX
Paper from
responsible sources
FSC® C104740

Sphere
An imprint of
Little, Brown Book Group
Carmelite House
50 Victoria Embankment
London EC4Y 0DZ

An Hachette UK Company
www.hachette.co.uk

www.littlebrown.co.uk

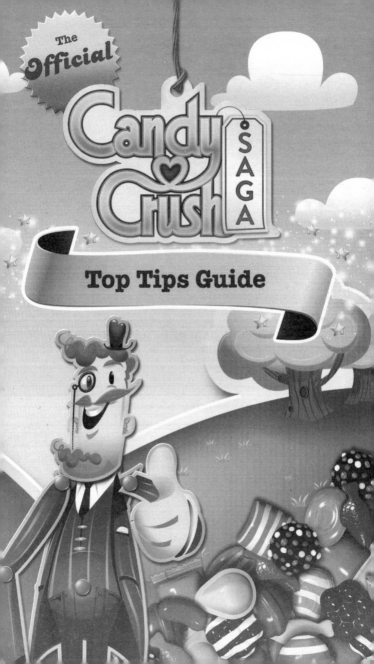

 Contents

What is Candy Crush Saga?

The Candy Crush franchise is one of the most successful casual gaming brands of its time with millions of players around the world. Offering fun, colourful and snackable gameplay, the original game, Candy Crush Saga, has been developed to be enjoyed by anyone, anytime, anywhere, when looking for some entertainment to brighten up the day!

In Candy Crush Saga, you switch and match colourful Candies to form epic, delicious chain reactions. You'll set off explosive boosters, causing Candies to cascade down the equally sweet game board. But you'll also have to engage your brain and implement your best strategies to clear the most devious of blockers and obstacles.

You can play Candy Crush Saga virtually anywhere including Google Android, iOS, Windows and Kindle devices, as well as Facebook and King.com. You can connect all of these accounts via Facebook too, so you'll never lose your progress.

Candy Crush Saga is set in the magically tasty world of the Candy Kingdom. It is here we meet our quirky yet extremely knowledgeable guide Mr. Toffee who runs the Candy Store in Candy Town.

One magical day in Candy Town, Mr. Toffee opened his delicious store to find a little candy bag had been left on his doorstep. To his delight, inside the bag he found a little bundle of sweetness called Tiffi, so he took her in and brought her up as his daughter. Tiffi is a humble girl and has lots of friends in Candy Town but is eager to explore more of the mesmerizing kingdom.

Under the watchful gaze of Mr. Toffee and alongside her great friend Yeti, she sets out to explore the Candy Kingdom. Her magical adventures take her to all sorts of wondrous places; the pretty Peppermint Palace, the lickable Lemonade Lake and the gorgeous Gingerbread Glade to name just a few. Along the way she stops to help some quirky characters and meets some even kookier animals, not to mention the mischievous Bubblegum Troll, who is intent on causing havoc in the Candy Kingdom! Follow Tiffi and her friends through delicious lands in your very own Candy Crush Saga.

Characters

Tiffi Toffee

Sweet little Tiffi was found in a candy bag and was brought up by Mr. Toffee in his Candy Store.

Tiffi loves to explore so she sets off through the Chocolate Mountains to begin her magical, candylicious adventures. Along her journey she stops to help some quirky characters and meets some even kookier animals, not to mention the mischievous Bubblegum Troll who always keeps her on her toes!

Mr. Toffee

Mr. Toffee is our quirky yet knowledgeable guide and mentor who runs the Candy Store in Candy Town. The magical day when Mr. Toffee found Tiffi was the best day of his life and since then he has dedicated much of his time teaching Tiffi about the Candy Kingdom.

He is worldly and intelligent, yet modest and is always happy to help point people in the right direction (quite literally) because that's just the nice kind of guy he is! Everyone loves Mr. Toffee not only because he's helpful but because he sells the best sweets in the whole of the Candy Kingdom.

Yeti

Yeti is Tiffi's best friend in the Candy Kingdom and is by her side through all her adventures.

He's definitely the coolest guy in Candy Town, so laid back he's practically horizontal! He's really likeable but a little slow to respond sometimes. Legend has it, it's because he's busy eating delicious Chocolates in his home in the Chocolate Mountains. It's really hard to stop, they are just so yummy!

Bubblegum Troll

No Candy Kingdom would be complete without a cheeky troublesome troll. Over the Easter Bunny Hills, lurking under the Bubblegum Bridge, you will find the naughty Bubblegum Troll! He's a cheeky little guy and always looking to try and sabotage Tiffi's helpful deeds for her friends. Though he's mischievous, he's quite kind really, so the people of Candy Kingdom love him. Sometimes he does come in quite useful in tricky situations.

Dragon

South of the Chocolate Mountains lies the Lemonade Lake, home to our friendly Dragon. He's the exception to the rule because he's happy, helpful and doesn't breathe fire. It's not that he doesn't want to, it's just that he can't! Living in the Lemonade Lake means that he's constantly drinking delicious sugary pop, so he's full of fizz rather than fire!

Worlds

Where would our colourful cast of characters be if they didn't have somewhere to call home?

Candy Kingdom
The magical land of the Candy Kingdom is where all of our action takes place! It's in this magical land where you'll spend your time adventuring, switching and matching your way past over 1000 challenging levels of bite-sized brilliance!

Candy Town
The famous Candy Town is home to the finest Candy Store in all of the Kingdom. It's here where our journey begins and where Tiffi sets off to start her epic quest across the Candy Kingdom. Candy Town is also the first episode of Candy Crush Saga, where Tiffi learns the basics and finds her feet before heading off into the vast expanse of the Candy Kingdom!

Chocolate Mountains
Chocolate Mountain is the fourth episode of Candy Crush Saga and it's also where you'll find Yeti. The Chocolate Mountains

are an amazing place, but they are not without hazards. Intrepid adventurers should best look out for the dreaded Liquorice Locks that can block your path leaving the Chocolate Mountains!

Lemonade Lake

Lemonade Lake is the home of the Dragon and the source of one of the tastiest beverages in all of the Candy Kingdom.

Bubblegum Bridge

The thing about bridges is that sometimes, nestled snugly underneath is a troll! Bubblegum Bridge is no exception, as this is where the ever annoying and sticky mess that is the Bubblegum Troll lives!

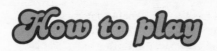

How to play

Candy Crush Saga is a match-three game where you'll have to look two, three and yes even four moves ahead. But for now let's start with the basics!

The aim of the game is to match three or more Candies of the same colour, which will set off a chain reaction causing the Candies to fall and cascade down the game board. Candies can be matched horizontally, vertically and sometimes across both, in either T or L formation.

How to Play:

Match three Candies of the same colour.

Like this:

Every level has its own specific objectives to clear the level. Objectives can vary depending on the level; they could be eliminating clear Jelly on the game board, collecting certain Ingredients, fulfilling Candy orders, or simply achieving a particular score! In each of these, you'll have a specific amount of moves or time in which to complete your objective.

If you fail to achieve the set objective before your moves are exhausted, you'll fail the level and lose a life. However, you can always ask your friends for help if you need a life – Delicious!

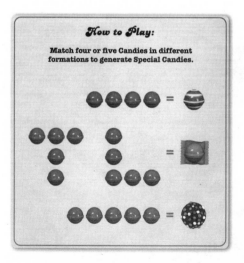

How to Play:

Match four or five Candies in different formations to generate Special Candies.

Special Candies

There are many Special Candies in Candy Crush Saga, each with their own unique effects! What's even better is that combining these Candies will create even more divine explosions!

Striped Candies

Striped Candies are one of the core Special Candies, and are extremely useful for getting you out of a sticky (or sweet) situation.

In order to create a Striped Candy, all you need to do is match four regular Candies in a row. There are two different types of Striped Candy: horizontal and vertical, and which one you receive depends on the orientation of your Candy match. So if you match four Candies

 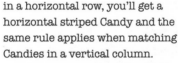 in a horizontal row, you'll get a horizontal striped Candy and the same rule applies when matching Candies in a vertical column.

To activate a striped Candy, match it with two or more Candies of the same colour. The result of this combination is an explosive one! The Striped Candy will clear a one-tile path through the game board – we call this combination a Line Blast.

  Striped Candies are great for several reasons; they can help you rack up big points, collect Candy orders, easily destroy Blockers and remove the clear Jelly. Their ability to clear rows and columns is also extremely helpful when you need to bring Ingredients down to the bottom of the game board.

Striped + Striped

When you combine two Striped Candies, two Line Blasts will activate; one horizontal and one vertical originating from where the combination was created – we call this combination a Double Line Blast.

Striped + Wrapped

When you combine a Striped Candy with a Wrapped Candy, a Line Blast will activate – but it will be three times as wide – a whole three tiles. This Line Blast will activate twice – firstly horizontally, then vertically. We call this combination a Super Line Blast.

Striped + Colour Bomb

When a Striped Candy is combined with a Colour Bomb, all Candies of the same colour will change into a Striped Candy and automatically activate.

Striped + Coconut Liquorice

When switched with a Striped Candy, the Coconut Liquorice will roll in the direction of the switch and create three Striped Candies. It will then appear on the opposite side of the board and create three more Striped Candies, which will automatically activate.

Striped + Swedish Fish

When combined with a Swedish Fish, the Candy will change into a Striped Swedish fish of the same colour, and proceed to swim off the game board. Three Striped Swedish Fish will swim back on to the board and change three regular Candies into Striped Candies that will then automatically activate.

Striped + UFO

When matched with a UFO, the Striped Candy will activate while the UFO takes flight; the UFO will then place three Wrapped Candies on the board, which will automatically activate.

Wrapped Candy

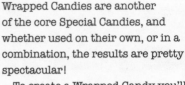

Wrapped Candies are another of the core Special Candies, and whether used on their own, or in a combination, the results are pretty spectacular!

To create a Wrapped Candy you'll have to match four Candies in either a T or L formation.

To activate a Wrapped Candy, match it with two or more Candies of the same colour. The result of this combination is quite powerful. The Wrapped Candy will explode (twice!), clearing all Candies in its blast radius – nine square tiles. We call this combination a Wrapped Explosion.

One of the cooler things about the Wrapped Candy is that when you activate one, you'll not only clear Blockers and unwanted Candies, but you'll also receive a ton of points, which can be especially helpful when a level's objective is score based!

Wrapped + Striped

When you combine a Wrapped Candy with a Striped Candy, a Line Blast will activate – but it will be three times as wide – a whole three tiles. This Line Blast will activate twice, firstly horizontally, then vertically. We call this combination a Super Line Blast.

Wrapped + Wrapped

When you combine two Wrapped Candies, the combination will result in a huge explosion clearing all Candies in its blast radius – a total of 24 tiles. We call this combination a Double Wrapped Explosion.

Wrapped + Colour Bomb

When a Wrapped Candy is combined with a Colour Bomb; the Colour Bomb will clear all Candies of the same colour, then randomly clear all Candies of another colour.

Wrapped + Coconut Liquorice

When a Coconut Liquorice is combined with a Wrapped Candy, the Wrapped Candy will first activate. Then, the Coconut Liquorice will roll off the screen in the direction of the switch and change every Candy in its path into a Wrapped Candy. It will return from the opposite side of the board and repeat the process. The Wrapped Candies automatically activate when the Coconut Liquorice is finished!

Wrapped + Swedish Fish

When combined with a Swedish Fish, the Wrapped Candy will change into a Wrapped Swedish Fish of the same colour, and swim off the game board. Three Wrapped Swedish Fish will swim back on to the board and change three regular Candies into Wrapped Candies that will then automatically activate.

Wrapped Candy + UFO

When matched with a UFO, the Wrapped Candy will activate while the UFO takes flight; the UFO will then place three Wrapped Candies on the board, which will automatically activate.

Colour Bomb

The Colour Bomb is definitely a Special Candy to watch out for!

Procuring one of these is fairly simple, all you need to do is match any five regular Candies of the same colour.

What makes the Colour Bomb so interesting? Activating a Colour Bomb will clear every Candy on the game board of any one colour; so if you match your Colour Bomb with a red Candy, all the red Candies on the game board will be destroyed!

To use the Colour Bomb, all you have to do is match it with any Candy of any colour! That is what makes this Candy so versatile, it doesn't have to be in a three-Candy match, any single Candy will activate it.

This can be super useful if you have an abundance of any one Candy, particularly in a Jelly level, but where the Colour Bomb really comes into its own is when it's matched with another Special Candy! The effects vary but can be extremely volatile, and in Candy Crush Saga, the more volatile, the better!

Colour Bomb + Striped

When a Colour Bomb is combined with a Striped Candy all regular Candies on the game board that are the same colour will be converted to Striped Candies and automatically activate.

Colour Bomb + Wrapped

When a Wrapped Candy is combined with a Colour Bomb; the Colour Bomb will clear all Candies of the same colour, then randomly clear all Candies of another colour.

Colour Bomb + Coconut Liquorice

When these two are combined, the Colour Bomb will target a random Candy and clear all Candies of the same colour. Even sweeter, the Coconut Liquorice will roll in the direction the switch was made (up, down, left or right), changing every Candy in its path into a Striped Candy. It will return from the opposite side of the game board and repeat the process. Quite a powerful combination!

Colour Bomb + Colour Bomb

When you combine two Colour Bombs, the result is electric! This powerful combination will clear the game board, activate all Special Candies and assist with clearing stubborn Blockers.

Colour Bomb + Swedish Fish

When a Colour Bomb is combined with a Swedish Fish the fish will take on the look of the Colour Bomb, and will then swim off the game board. Three 'Colour Bomb' Swedish Fish will swim back on to the game board and convert regular Candies to Swedish Fish. After this, each one of the newly created Swedish Fish will then activate.

Colour Bomb + UFO

When combined with a UFO, the Colour Bomb will target a random Candy, and all Candies of the same colour will be destroyed. At the same time, the UFO will place three wrapped Candies on the board, which will then activate simultaneously.

Coconut Liquorice

The Coconut Liquorice is a mouth-watering booster, sought after by many a Player. But this marvellous Booster can't be gained through successful matches. In order to utilize the benefits of the Coconut Liquorice you'll have to trade in gold bars. Although you can also get them through the Booster Wheel.

The Coconut Liquorice is extremely powerful and can create a cascade chain reaction of epic proportions. To activate it you'll need to switch it with any single Candy. Once switched, it will clear the Candy you switched it with, then the first three Candies in the direction you've switched (up, down, left, and right) will turn into striped Candies and activate.

You can easily see how this Candy can be extremely helpful in clearing vast amounts of Candies from the board. You not only get the benefits of clearing the switched Candy, you also get the three extra Striped Candies and the associated Line Blast combinations.

Another great thing about the Coconut Liquorice is when you combine it with another Special Candy, the reactions can sometimes clear the entire board, which can make the Coconut Liquorice the nuclear option of Special Candies!

Coconut Liquorice + Striped Candy

When switched with a Striped Candy, the Coconut Liquorice will roll in the direction of the switch and create three Striped Candies. It will then appear on the opposite side of the board and create three more Striped Candies, which will automatically activate.

Coconut Liquorice + Wrapped Candy

When a Coconut Liquorice is combined with a Wrapped Candy, the Wrapped Candy will first activate. Following this, the Coconut Liquorice will roll off the screen in the direction of the switch and change every Candy in its path into a Wrapped Candy. It will return from the opposite side of the board and repeat the process. The Wrapped Candies will automatically activate when the Coconut Liquorice is finished!

Coconut Liquorice + Colour Bomb

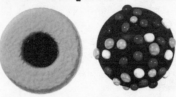

When these two are combined, the Colour Bomb will target a random Candy and clear all Candies of the same colour. Even sweeter, the Coconut Liquorice will roll in the direction the switch was made (up, down, left or right), changing every Candy in its path into a Striped Candy. It will return from the opposite side of the game board and repeat the process. Quite a powerful combination!

Coconut Liquorice + UFO

When combined with a UFO, the Coconut Liquorice will activate first and create three Striped Candies as if it was matched with a regular Candy. Once the board stabilises, the UFO will then create three Wrapped Candies.

Swedish Fish

When it comes to Jelly levels, the Swedish Fish can greatly improve your chances of clearing the level. Swedish Fish thrive on consuming clear Jelly – a very handy Booster, indeed.

To activate them you'll need to create a match with three or more Candies, or by hitting it with a line or Wrapped Candy blast or even a combination of the two! Once activated, a Swedish Fish will swim across the game board and out of sight. After this, three more of his Swedish Fish friends - not wanting to be left out - will swim across the game board and fill their bellies with clear Jelly.

Swedish Fish are useful for the obvious reasons; if you can activate one you'll give yourself a chance to eliminate those pesky hard to reach clear Jellies. They can also help you get rid of some of the more stubborn blockers: such as Liquorice and Liquorice Locks, providing that clear Jelly is lurking behind them.

When it comes to Frosting, Swedish Fish will consume the clear Jelly that lies underneath.

As with all Special Candies, combining Swedish Fish with another Special Candy can create even greater effects with the potential to consume the majority of the clear Jelly on screen, depending on the Special Candy it's mixed with!

Swedish Fish + Striped

When combined with a Swedish Fish, the Striped Candy will change into a Striped Swedish Fish of the same colour, and proceed to swim off the game board. Three Striped Swedish Fish will swim back on to the board and change three regular Candies into Striped Candies that will then automatically activate.

Swedish Fish + Wrapped

When combined with a Swedish Fish, the Wrapped Candy will change into a Wrapped Swedish Fish of the same colour, and proceed to swim off the game board. Three Wrapped Swedish Fish will swim back on to the game board and change three regular Candies into Wrapped Candies that will then automatically activate.

Swedish Fish + Colour Bomb

When a Colour Bomb is combined with a Swedish Fish it will gain sprinkles, much like the Colour Bomb, and will then swim off the game board. Three sprinkled Swedish Fish will swim back on to the game board and change regular Candies to Swedish Fish. After this, each one of the newly created Swedish Fish will then activate.

Swedish Fish + UFO

When combined with a UFO, the Swedish Fish will swim across the game board and out of sight. Three more Swedish Fish will swim onto the game board and remove the clear Jelly. After the game board stabilizes, the UFO will then place three Wrapped Candies on the board.

Mystery Candy

The Mystery Candy is everything and nothing all at once, quantum entanglement, the mysteries of the universe all encapsulated in one glorious bundle of infinite possibility! To crack it open, you'll need to create a match with regular Candies of the same colour.

The devious thing about the Mystery Candy is that when you finally manage to crack one open, it can transform into an awesome Special Candy or booster, or it could blow up in your face and turn into something far more horrible, like the dreaded Multi Layered Frosting!

Every swipe of the Mystery Candy is an adventure into the unknown – good luck!

UFO

The UFO is definitely out of this world and one of the more powerful Special Candies! The UFO is easy to spot; look for a spinning pink Candy that causes delectable damage once activated.

To activate the UFO, all you need to do is switch it with any Candy (up, down, left and right). Once activated, the UFO will hover over the board and convert three Candies to Wrapped Candies – score! These Wrapped Candies will then activate, causing Candies to cascade down the game board.

UFO + Striped Candy

When matched with a UFO, the Striped Candy will activate while the UFO takes flight; the UFO will then place three Wrapped Candies on the board, which will automatically activate.

UFO + Wrapped Candy

When matched with a UFO, the Wrapped Candy will activate while the UFO takes flight; the UFO will then place three Wrapped Candies on the board, which will automatically activate.

UFO + Colour Bomb

When combined with a UFO the Colour Bomb will activate while the UFO takes flight; the UFO will then place three Wrapped Candies on the board, which will automatically activate.

UFO + Coconut Liquorice

When combined with a UFO the Coconut Liquorice will activate first and create three striped Candies as if it was matched with a regular Candy. Once the board stabilises, the UFO will then place three Wrapped Candies on the board, which will automatically activate.

UFO + Swedish Fish

When combined with a UFO, the Swedish Fish will swim across the game board and out of sight. Three more Swedish Fish will swim onto the game board and remove the clear Jelly. After the game board stabilizes, the UFO will then place three Wrapped Candies on the board.

Boosters

Boosters are a helping hand that can get you out of a jam. If you've got one clear Jelly left on the board and only one move to spare, or need to set up a huge combination to achieve a point score, a booster can be a welcome addition to your Candy Crush Saga arsenal.

Lucky Candy

Sometimes to pass a particularly tricky level, you need a little luck. Available as a booster for order fulfilment levels, the Lucky Candy can provide just the helping hand you need to clear a level. When you select this booster, a Lucky Candy will be added to the game board, and will be available to match with regular Candies. When you use the Lucky Candy to make a successful match, it will release a Candy to the game board – this Candy will be just the thing you need to clear the objective, and the level.

Lollipop Hammer

The Lollipop Hammer is one of the most useful and versatile boosters. This deliciously pink Lollipop has the final say, as it launches itself onto the game board, clearing the most stubborn of Blockers and stray Candies.

If you find yourself down to your last move, with one stray Candy or Blocker standing between you and glory; the Lollipop Hammer can be activated to clear that final Candy in one mighty move.

You can get the Lollipop Hammer by trading in gold bars or in the Booster Wheel.

Extra Moves (+5)

Picture this, you've defeated the Frosting, beat the Candy Bomb and unlocked the Sugar Chests. You can see the light at the end of the tunnel; only two more clear Jellies to clear the level!

But then the dread grabs you; you've only got one move left. But wait, there's a way – surely! You've got it, it's Extra Moves! If you find yourself at the end of your move allocation, you can use the Extra Moves Booster to gain an additional five moves and continue the level. You can obtain the Extra Moves Booster by trading in gold bars!

Extra Time

Extra Time works much like the Extra Moves booster. If you are in a timed level and see the clock ticking down a little faster than you would like, you can use this booster to give you a little more time in which to clear the level.

This booster can only be used in timed levels, and can be gained by trading in gold bars.

Free Switcher Hand

Sometimes you can see a match that could be a game-changer - if only that red Candy was one tile to the left. Well my friend, there is a way to make that perfect, successful match, and it's only a Booster away.

The Free Switcher Hand allows you to bypass the normal rules of Candy Crush Saga and switch two adjacent Candies, even if they don't match! If you need to reposition a green Candy so you can set up a huge combo, you can go right on ahead.

What's even better is that the Free Switcher Hand does not take up a move, so you can set up that perfect match without having to worry about Chocolate Spawning, or the Toffee Tornado shifting.

The Free Switch can be gained by trading in gold bars.

Striped + Wrapped

This booster gives you a head start before you've even started the level. When you activate it you'll start your level with both a Wrapped and Striped Candy.

So if you're stuck on a particularly tricky level, keep running out of moves or time or want to clear as many Candies as you can; this is your Booster of choice. You can gain this by trading in gold bars.

Sweet Teeth

The Sweet Teeth is the in-game manifestation of your subconscious desire to devour all the Candy in the Candy Crush Saga Universe.

Once activated, this hungry booster will chew its way through the sweetest route, and devour the Candies that you need to clear as a priority – it will aim to remove clear Jelly on Jelly levels, any Candies that are inhibiting you collecting Ingredients, and of course blockers. So, if you have a nightmare game board full of Liquorice Locks and Chocolate, activate the Sweet Teeth for a sweet boost.

Bomb Cooler

The dreaded Candy Bomb takes a lot of time and effort to clear and tests the luck and multi-tasking skills of the most enthusiastic players. One forgotten Candy Bomb left to explode, and the result is a premature end to the level. The Bomb Cooler Booster gives you the opportunity to stop that from happening, at least for a short period.

Using the Bomb Cooler will give you extra time to defuse what could be an extremely explosive situation! For any Candy Bombs on the game board; the Bomb Cooler will add an extra five moves to the countdown timer. For example, if a Candy Bomb has three moves left before it explodes, using the Bomb Cooler will award five extra moves which means the Candy Bomb now has eight moves before it explodes.

This is a supremely useful booster and can be gained by trading in gold bars.

Blockers

Take a moment to picture yourself surrounded by Chocolate, Frosting, Cake, and more Chocolate. Sounds absolutely delicious, doesn't it? Well, in the Candy Kingdom it's not as sweet as it sounds. If you encounter any of these divine delights, you're up against the bothersome Blockers. As challenging as they can be, defeating them is so much sweeter.

Clear Jelly

The first five levels of Candy Crush are a tantalising introduction to the world of Candy Kingdom. To make the experience even sweeter, you'll discover a delicious new challenge from level six onwards – clear Jelly. When you encounter a level with clear Jelly, the objective is to remove all the clear Jelly before you exhaust your allocated moves. Clear Jelly has a translucent appearance, and will be positioned behind a Candy. As you make moves, and Candies move down the game board, the clear Jelly will remain on the tile (unless you clear it of course!). Keep an eye out for the double clear Jelly. With two layers of jiggly clear Jelly to remove, you'll need to implement your best strategies to clear the level.

✷ Make a match with a Candy on a clear Jelly tile ✷ Activate a Line Blast, Double Line Blast, Super Line Blast, Wrapped Explosion, or Double Wrapped Explosion in the path of the clear Jelly ✷ Activate a Colour Bomb with a corresponding Candy positioned on a clear Jelly tile

Activating a Swedish Fish booster on the board will generate three swimming Swedish Fish that will remove three random clear Jelly tiles – even the clear Jelly behind the Multi Layered Frosting.

Frosting

After breezing through the first 20 levels, you'll come up against a new challenge – the delectable, creamy blocker Frosting. Frosting will occupy one tile, and cannot be moved or switched with Candies.

✷ Make a match adjacent to the Frosting ✷ Activate a Line Blast, Double Line Blast, Super Line Blast, Wrapped Explosion, or Double Wrapped Explosion in the path of the Frosting

✹ The ever helpful Colour Bomb can't help you defeat the Frosting - any Frosting adjacent to Candies cleared by a Colour Bomb will remain on the board

---

Because you've mastered the skills to clear Frosting, a new challenge will be set for you from Level 111: Multi Layered Frosting. You can employ all the same strategies used to clear Frosting, but as this Frosting has multiple layers, you'll need to repeat the process until you've completely cleared the tile. As more focus is required to clear Multi Layered Frosting, you can now activate a Colour Bomb to assist you with this task. Try activating a Colour Bomb to clear Candies adjacent to the Multi Layered Frosting - one layer of Frosting will be cleared, getting you one step closer to defeating the Frosting!

Liquorice Lock

Making its first appearance in Level 25; the Liquorice Lock is a somewhat stubborn Blocker and cannot be moved or switched with Candies. Even the most skilled of Candy Crush Saga players find Liquorice Locks to be a challenge. You'll find no better example of this obstacle than the notorious Level 65, which tests the skills, luck and patience of all Candy Crush Saga players. There are multiple ways to rid the board game of Liquorice Locks, but just remember once you clear the Liquorice Lock, the Candy underneath will remain (and in some cases there may still be clear Jelly to remove).

Liquorice

What's better than Liquorice? A double dose of Liquorice! After the introduction of the Liquorice Lock, come these luscious swirls of Liquorice. This moveable blocker can be switched with an adjacent Candy to create a match, however matching three or more Liquorice will not result in their removal. But, Liquorice does not duplicate, unlike our friend Chocolate (more on that later).

Chocolate and Chocolate Fountains

For most people, the concept of self-replicating Chocolate would be a dream come true – delicious, creamy chocolate squares populating every corner and crevice of your world. However, in the world of Candy Crush Saga, Chocolate is the enemy. First seen in Level 51; Chocolate grows and expands across the game board if you don't clear it. If no Chocolate is cleared when you make a match, Chocolate will duplicate in a random adjacent cell.

TRY THIS

✳ Make a match adjacent to the Chocolate ✳ Activate a Line Blast, Double Line Blast, Super Line Blast, Wrapped Explosion, or Double Wrapped Explosion in the path of the Chocolate ✳ Activate a Colour Bomb so that it clears a Candy adjacent to the Chocolate

---

Moving on to level 156, and you've mastered the art of clearing all the Chocolate. You're making matches, busting moves, and resisted all temptation to eat the real thing.

You're now up against the Chocolate Fountain. The Chocolate Fountain remains on the board for the duration of the level, and cannot be removed or moved. Its one goal is to make sure your Chocolate cravings are satisfied – if at any stage, there is no Chocolate on the game board, the Chocolate Fountain will spawn Chocolate after two moves. If there is Chocolate on the game board; one of two things will happen – the existing Chocolate on the game board will replicate if not cleared via a match, or the Chocolate Fountain will spawn new Chocolate.

Marmalade

This beloved breakfast preserve makes its (unofficial) first appearance in level 70, but that's just a sample of what's to come. You'll see more of Marmalade from level 187, and it's got something to hide!

Hidden behind Marmalade, you'll usually find a sweet treat – usually in the form of a Special Candy, a Booster, or something more mysterious... However, it's not always the best strategy to clear the Marmalade as a priority. If you wait to clear the Marmalade, its contents may benefit you when your moves are limited.

TRY THIS

* Make a match adjacent to the Marmalade
* Activate a Line Blast or Wrapped Explosion in the path of the Marmalade

---

Cake Bomb

Making its delicious debut in level in Level 366, the Cake Bomb is a blocker that requires focus to clear. Covering a total of four tiles, this mouthwatering sweet treat is divided into eight segments. To clear the Cake Bomb, you will need to clear all eight segments. Once cleared, the party gets started with a party popper clearing the board!

TRY THIS

✹ Make a match adjacent to the Cake Bomb. The Cake Bomb segment adjacent to the match will be cleared ✹ Activating a Line Blast can clear up to two segments from the Cake Bomb – one from each quadrant in the path of the striped Candy ✹ Activating a Wrapped Explosion is the most effective of the Special Candies – if detonated adjacent to the Cake Bomb, it has the ability to clear up to four segments within the blast radius ✹ Activating a Double Wrapped Explosion adjacent to a Cake Bomb has the ability to clear up to all eight segments within the blast radius ✹ Activating a Super Line Blast in the path of the Cake Bomb can clear up to four segments – one from each quadrant in the combination's path ✹ Activating a 'Colour Bomb + Wrapped Candy/Striped Candy/Colour Bomb' blast is also extremely helpful – it can result in all eight segments being cleared.

Sugar Chest

Locked away until level 711,
this delightful blocker needs
a key just as sweet to release
its contents. Sugar Chests
will remain on the board
until a match is made with a
Sugar Key and two or more
corresponding Candies. Once you make this match,
the Sugar Key will open the Sugar Chest and the
contents will be in play on the game board.

However, sometimes Sugar Chests are made even
sweeter by the addition of multiple layers of crumbly
biscuit, gooey jam and sticky icing. You'll need to
make multiple matches with Sugar Keys to clear
these layers before the Sugar Chest opens.

Candy Bomb

Level 100 is in your sights. You can almost taste it. Hold off on celebrating though, because from level 96 onwards you're up against a new blocker – the Candy Bomb. The Candy Bomb is here to test your best strategies, and your good fortune. The timer on the Candy Bomb represents how many moves are available before the Candy Bomb explodes and the game is over. To clear the Candy Bomb, and ensure your game isn't ended prematurely:

TRY THIS

✻ Make a match with a Candy Bomb and two or more corresponding Candies ✻ Activate a Line Blast, Double Line Blast, Super Line Blast, Wrapped Explosion, or Double Wrapped Explosion in the path of the Candy Bomb ✻ Activate a Colour Bomb with a Candy of the corresponding colour ✻ Use a Candy Bomb Cooler to add an additional five moves to the Candy Bombs on the board ✻ Watch out for Candy Bombs behind Liquorice Locks – the timer will still continue to count down. So make sure you clear that Liquorice lock before the Candy Bomb explodes!

Popcorn

The familiar smell of buttery, crunchy popcorn fills the air from Level 771. This stationery (but oh-so-appetising) blocker can only be cleared by activating Line Blasts, Double Line Blasts, Super Line Blasts, Wrapped Explosions, or Double Wrapped Explosions.

However, it will take more than attempt to clear from the board. On the first and second attempt, the popcorn will grow in size, until the third attempt where it will make one final pop and reveal a Colour Bomb.

NOTE: Popcorn is immune to the Lollipop Hammer.

Other Elements

Ingredients: Cherry and Hazelnut

Our favourite purveyor of all things delicious and divine, Mr. Toffee, understands the importance of collecting the finest ingredients. From Level 11 onwards, your next challenge is to collect the Ingredients including the delectable hazelnuts and the moreish cherries. Keep an eye on the Ingredients tally; this will be your reference point for how many Ingredients you need to collect to meet the objective and clear the level.

NOTE: Ingredients can't move past blockers – make sure you clear the blockers first to ensure a clear passage to the bottom of the game board.

Teleporter

Step in to the future with the Teleporter – seen from level 66 onwards. As Candies move and cascade down the game board, they'll move through the Blue Teleporter, and re-enter via the Pink Teleporter.

Frog

This sticky-footed Candy Frog loves to eat Candies! To appease its appetite, match the Candy Frog with two Candies of the same colour. Once the Candy Frog's belly is full, you'll be able to select the Candy Frog, and move it to another position on the game board. From the Candy Frog's new position, it will clear all adjacent Candies and blockers.

TRY THIS

Try these Frogtastic matches! ✳ Matching four Candies in a row or column - including a Candy Frog - creates a Striped Frog ✳ Matching four Candies in a T or L shape - including a Candy Frog - creates a Wrapped Frog ✳ Matching five Candies in a row or column - including a Candy Frog - creates a Colour Bomb Frog

TIP: If a Striped or Wrapped Frog is on the game board when you activate a Colour Bomb with a Candy of the same colour, the Striped or Wrapped Candy Frog will immediately activate.

Combine a Candy Frog and a Special Candy (Striped, Wrapped, or Colour Bomb) and the Candy Frog will not only activate the Special Candy, but take on the form of the matched Special Candy.

Conveyor Belt

A sweet new challenge in the form of the Conveyor Belt awaits you from level 531. Always on the move, this luscious liquorice Conveyor Belt can move vertically or horizontally, around corners, and through its own teleporter. Keep an eye on the directional arrows on the Conveyor Belt – for every successful match made, the conveyer belt will move ahead one tile.

Switchable items such as Candies, Special Candies, Liquorice, Coconut Liquorices and Ingredients can find their way on to the Conveyor Belt, so keep an eye out for opportunities to make some extra Special matches as the Conveyor Belt makes its way around the board.

Although it sounds delicious, you won't see Frosting, Chocolate or Toffee Tornadoes land on, or move via the Conveyor Belt – phew!

Chameleon Candies

Your eyes aren't deceiving you; the dazzling, vibrant aura you see from level 306 is real, and it's called the Chameleon Candy. Encased by its rainbow glow, the Chameleon Candy has all the same matching capabilities as a normal Candy – with one additional characteristic. After every move you make on the game board, the Chameleon Candy will change to an alternate Candy colour.

Toffee Tornado

Take cover! Coming straight for you at Level 411 is the Toffee Tornado. This indestructible blocker has the ability to move - quickly! For every other successful match you make on the board, the Toffee Tornado will move to a new random tile. If there is Candy or Mystery Candy on the tile, say goodbye to it! If there is a Special Candy on the tile, watch it activate! If there is a blocker on the tile, the blocker will lose one layer (handy if it's Frosting).

Toffee Tornadoes cannot move to tiles that contain any of the below:
Cake Bomb, Ingredients such as Hazelnut or Cherry, Another Toffee Tornado, Chocolate Fountain, Coconut Liquorice, Lucky Candy

There are some powerful combinations you can employ for some instant relief. By activating any of the below combinations in the path of the Toffee Tornado, it will twist its way off the board for good!
Line Blast, Double Line Blast, Super Line Blast, Wrapped Explosion, Double Wrapped Explosion, Cake Bomb Blast

Tips for Tricky

DREAMWORLD: Level 70

FOCUS ON

ODUS will fall easily in this level. Keep the Moon Scale as stable as you can! On the left side of the game board, try to create as many Special Candies as you can, but wait to activate them until Moon Struck, when the Moon Scale is no longer a worry. If you can clear the Chocolate, do it!

WATCH OUT FOR

WHEN CLEARING Chocolate, make sure you don't open the Liquorice Locks until all of the Chocolate is cleared. If you do, the Chocolate will duplicate out of control and take over the right side of the game board.

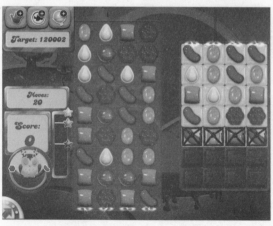

DREAMWORLD: Level 73

FOCUS ON

CHOCOLATE! When the second Moon Struck hits you should have aimed to have cleared all the Chocolate.

WATCH OUT FOR

THE VERY unstable Moon Scale – Odus will fall easily!

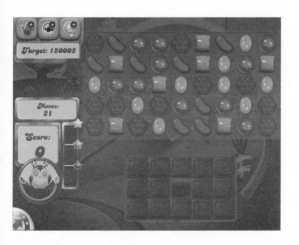

DREAMWORLD: Level 101

FOCUS ON ACTIVATING LINE Blasts and Wrapped Explosions – they're very helpful when you want to quickly bring down ingredients.

WATCH OUT FOR THE VERY unstable Moon Scale – Odus will fall easily! It's also advised to keep an eye on the Candy Bombs.

DREAMWORLD: Level 104

FOCUS ON

YOUR FIRST priority should be to remove the Candy Bombs. If possible activate a vertical Line Blast, as you'll clear extra blockers with the one move.

WATCH OUT FOR

A RISKY combination of few too moves, and Moon Scale will cause an unstable Odus. Make sure he doesn't fall!

Don't forget the Chocolate too – make sure you keep your eye on it!

DREAMWORLD: Level 130

FOCUS ON

ALL YOUR effort should go into creating Striped Candies and activating as many combinations are you can. Think twice before you make your move - this level doesn't give you very many moves to start with and they are all vital.

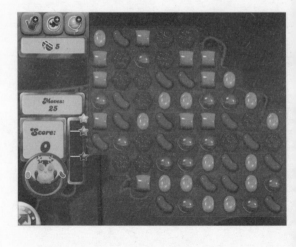

DREAMWORLD: Level 168

FOCUS ON

IT'S EASY to start worrying about the Candy Bombs too early on this level - don't. You have 13 moves before they explode, and Chocolate might just be the helping hand you need. As the Chocolate replicates and grows, it may just grow over those Candy Bombs.

Liquorice Locks and the Multi Layered Frosting should be your main priority from the start, since the clear Jelly you need to remove is underneath that Frosting. Line Blasts and Wrapped Explosions will be very helpful to clear the board as fast as possible.

WATCH OUT FOR

DON'T ACTIVATE a Colour Bomb until you've cleared the Liquorice Locks – once you've done this, the Multi Layered Frosting will be easily cleared.

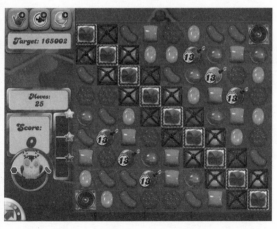

DREAMWORLD: Level 195

 FOCUS ON LINE BLASTS, Double Line Blasts, Super Line Blasts, Wrapped Explosions, and Double Wrapped Explosions – make as many special combinations as you can!

 WATCH OUT FOR AVOID CLEARING the Marmalade and activating the Wrapped Candies until you have an opportunity to create a combination with Striped Candies.

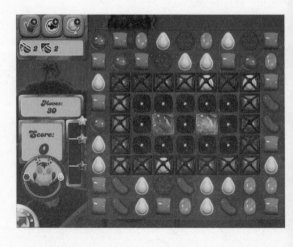

DREAMWORLD: Level 237

FOCUS ON

CLEARING THAT pesky Chocolate while trying to create as many Striped Candies as you can.

WATCH OUT FOR

THE MOON Struck! It can activate any Special Candies prematurely – throwing out any future plans you had for them.

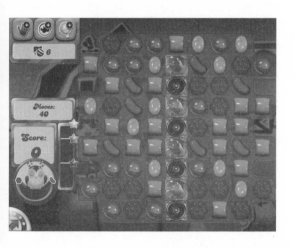

DREAMWORLD: Level 289

FOCUS ON

CLEARING THOSE Blockers, and opening up the board! Keep your focus on the middle of the board.

WATCH OUT FOR

MAKE SURE to keep an eye on Odus to ensure he doesn't fall. Avoid activating any Colour Bombs while not in Moon Struck.

DREAMWORLD: Level 376

FOCUS ON

YOUR FIRST priority should be clearing the Cake Bomb. Following that, focus on clearing the Frosting. When both are cleared, dedicate your remaining moves to bring the Ingredients down.

WATCH OUT FOR

DON'T WASTE all your moves clearing Chocolate. It's easy to fall in to that trap and focusing solely on the Chocolate, but on this level in particular the Cake Bomb is King!

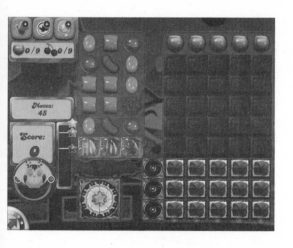

DREAMWORLD: Level 384

FOCUS ON
YOUR MAIN focus should be ensuring Odus is balanced and doesn't fall.

WATCH OUT FOR
UTILIZE MOON Struck to clear Candy Bombs. Don't be too eager to unlock the Marmalade all at once – you may need to utilize the Special Candies later in the game.

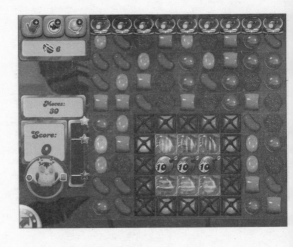

DREAMWORLD: Level 385

FOCUS ON
CLEARING OUT the lower half of the game board with the help of Special Candies, preferably vertical Striped Candies.

WATCH OUT FOR
THE MYSTERY Candy – it can lead to both glory and defeat. If the result is a blocker, prioritize in clearing it ASAP!

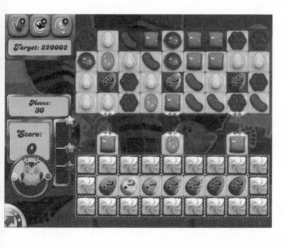

DREAMWORLD: Level 395

THE MOON Scale – it's highly unstable!

FOCUS ON

AS TEMPTING as it is to open up the whole game board by clearing both the Liquorice and Frosting, the result will be Odus falling. Keep an eye on which side the first Ingredient appears from the Candy Cannon – this should be the side you focus on clearing. Employing this strategy will ensure the Candy Cannon on the opposite side of the game board doesn't dispense unwanted ingredients.

WATCH OUT FOR

Save any Colour Bombs and Striped Candies for Moon Struck. If possible, activate a Colour Bomb and Striped Candy combination to bring down several ingredients at once.

DREAMWORLD: Level 409

FOCUS ON TRY TO create matches that result in the Ingredients moving to one side of the game board. That way, you only need to focus on clearing one Cake Bomb to collect your ingredients.

WATCH OUT FOR CLEARING THE Marmalade and using those Striped Candies too soon - save it for that one last piece of the delicious Cake Bomb.

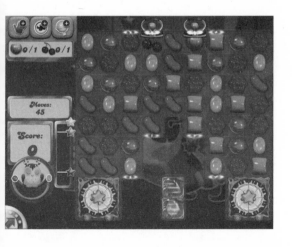

DREAMWORLD: Level 430

FOCUS ON

CLEARING THE Marmalade and activating the Colour Bombs immediately. With so few moves, there's no time to waste! If possible, try to activate a Colour Bomb and Wrapped Candy combination.

WATCH OUT FOR

THERE'S A lot of elements to this level that could result in failure, and fast! Candy Bombs: remove them as soon as you can! Chocolate: keep it under control! As for activating a Colour Bomb, make sure to keep an eye on the Moon Scale – Odus could fall easily.

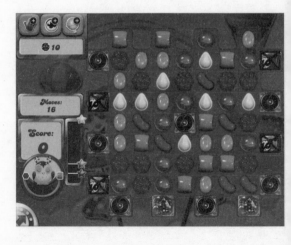

DREAMWORLD: Level 541

FOCUS ON

CLEARING THE Candy Bombs before the first Moon Struck.

WATCH OUT FOR

THE VERY unstable Moon Scale – Odus will fall easily! Be careful when activating Special Candies and combinations – this could tip Odus over the edge.

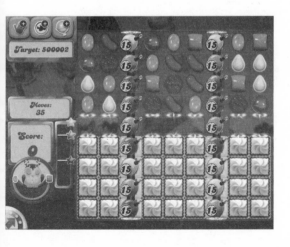

DREAMWORLD: Level 585

FOCUS ON

MAKING MATCHES to create the right Special Candies at the right time. A Super Line Blast is ideal on this level since it can tear through Candy Bombs and Liquorice.

WATCH OUT FOR

THE CANDY Bombs - keep a close eye on their timers!

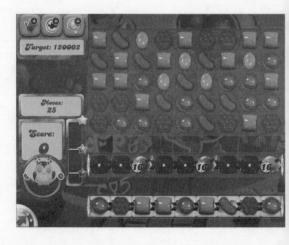

DREAMWORLD: Level 587

PRIORITIZE MAKING strategic moves
and matches to create Striped Candies.
Activate them to bring down Ingredients
quickly and efficiently – one row at a time.

KEEP ONE eye on the Moon Scale. Even
though you may feel confident with the
number of moves allotted, don't forget
about Odus!

CANDY KINGDOM: LEVEL 86

FOCUS ON

DON'T EXHAUST moves on clearing Liquorice and Liquorice Locks. Utilize your available moves by making matches to create Striped and Wrapped Candies and activating combinations to clear the Blockers. Even more beneficial is the coveted Colour Bomb + Colour Bomb combination.

WATCH OUT FOR

MAKE SURE you don't focus on or prioritize one side of the game board. You'll need to tackle the clear Jelly in the corners from all angles.

CANDY KINGDOM: Level 105

FOCUS ON

PRIORITIZE CLEARING the Liquorice Lock in the centre of the game board. The timer on the Candy Bomb underneath it will continue to count down, so make sure you clear it before it's too late. Next priority – remove that clear Jelly, as it's the key to passing the level.

WATCH OUT FOR

MORE CANDY Bombs will continue to fall. Make sure to keep an eye on their count down timers.

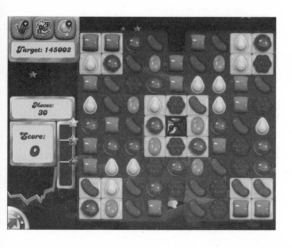

CANDY KINGDOM: Level 125

REMOVING THE clear Jelly by activating Line Blasts and Wrapped Explosions.

CLEAR THE game board from as much Liquorice as you can – they take up precious tile space, and they can block the effect of some combinations.

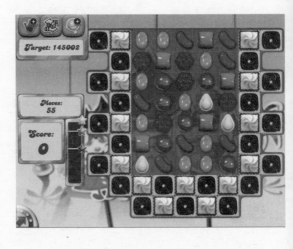

CANDY KINGDOM: Level 140

FOCUS ON

IT'S TIME to start collecting, and nothing is more efficient at the task than the Colour Bomb. Match a Colour Bomb with a Candy that you don't need to collect – its removal from the game board will cause cascades that will assist you in the task of collecting Candies you need.

WATCH OUT FOR

TRY TO keep an even variation of different Candies on the board. You don't want to exhaust one type of Candy while on your last few moves.

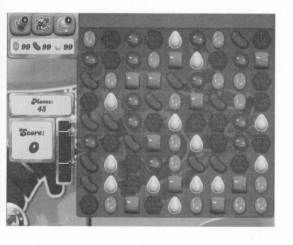

CANDY KINGDOM: Level 168

FOCUS ON

IMPLEMENT A strategy of speed and efficiency to overcome this level. Endeavour to bring the ingredients down and to the right side of the game board soon as you can. Activate Line Blasts and Wrapped Explosions to clear large sections of the level at the same time.

WATCH OUT FOR

CHOCOLATE. CHOCOLATE everywhere! This level has two Chocolate Fountains, so it can easily and quickly replicate out of control.

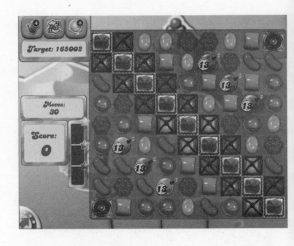

CANDY KINGDOM: Level 201

FOCUS ON ACTIVATING LINE Blasts and Wrapped Explosions – they're incredibly helpful for clearing multiple clear Jellies at the same time, including the tricky hard-to-reach clear Jellies in the disconnected tiles.

WATCH OUT FOR MAKE SURE every move counts, as clear Jelly occupies every tile on this level.

CANDY KINGDOM: Level 245

FOCUS ON

MAKE STRATEGIC moves to create a Colour Bomb. Once available, activate the Colour Bomb with the Candy that has the highest quantity on the game board. This will allow a cascade effect that may result in a higher number of Special Candies.

WATCH OUT FOR

TAKE YOUR time and proceed with caution before making a move as you may inadvertently activate a Special Candy that would have been beneficial for future moves.

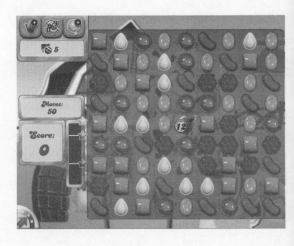

CANDY KINGDOM: Level 266

FOCUS ON

PRIORITIZE CREATING striped Candies on the top half of the game board so as to avoid the Candy Cannons and the Candy Bombs it will begin to dispense. It's not just Candy Bombs you have to worry about in the bottom half of the game board - avoid cascades that may inadvertently activate your striped Candies before you have the chance to make strategic combinations.

WATCH OUT FOR

CANDY BOMBS released from the Candy Cannon will have 15 moves before they explode, so when you have 15 or less moves remaining you can stop worry about them being dispensed. Clear the Chocolate as fast as possible, don't let it grow out of control!

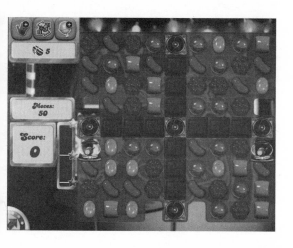

CANDY KINGDOM: Level 273

FOCUS ON

CLEARING THE Frosting and Multi Layered Frosting to access those hard-to-reach clear Jellies. Your best strategy is to create and activate vertical Line Blasts to clear the dreaded Candy Bombs.

WATCH OUT FOR

THE CANDY Bombs countdown timer – these Candy Bombs have a short fuse, so make sure you clear them before they explode and it's game over!

CANDY KINGDOM: Level 305

FOCUS ON — PRIORITY IS to break down the Frosting quickly, so you can tackle the Multi Layered Frosting, and finally the clear Jelly it's blocking.

WATCH OUT FOR — MYSTERY CANDY! Sure, they can be a great help, but they also have the ability to turn a nice level into a nasty one. Proceed with care...

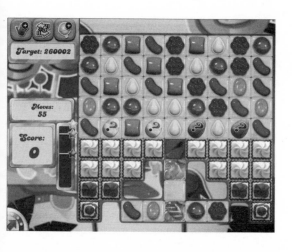

CANDY KINGDOM: Level 323

FOCUS ON KEEP YOUR eyes peeled for Mystery Candy. The optimal way to clear this level is to create a Colour Bomb from a Mystery Candy and then activating with a striped Candy. A Super Line Blast is also incredibly helpful to clear those disconnected tiles.

WATCH OUT FOR AN ALMOST empty lower half of the game board, where no matches are available. If you find yourself in this predicament, only a vertical Line Blast can help you.

CANDY KINGDOM: Level 345

THIS IS a challenging level for many reasons: the high number of orders to collect, the hard-to-get-to Candy Bombs, and not to mention it features all six Candy colours!

Focus on clearing the Candy Bombs first. This is best achieved by creating a number of striped Candies to create Line Blasts.

Try a Colour Bomb and Striped Candy combination – this will assist you in collecting your order quickly and efficiently, as well as clearing any Candy Bombs left behind.

CANDY KINGDOM: Level 347

FOCUS ON

SPECIAL CANDIES are key here – prioritize creating and activating Wrapped Candies, as they will assist in fulfilling the order and create further matches through any cascades.

WATCH OUT FOR

THE MULTI Layered Frosting – leave it be if you can, as it blocks the Chocolate Fountain from creating havoc.

CANDY KINGDOM: Level 365

All six Candy colours, limited space and substantial orders make this level quite a challenge!

FOCUS ON

CLEARING THE Frosting and Multi Level Frosting to allow extra room for creating Striped and Wrapped Candies. When it comes to the Chameleon Candy, only make matches if it assists in fulfilling orders.

WATCH OUT FOR

AS YOUR moves are depleted, don't place too much emphasis on clearing the Frosting and Multi Layered Frosting. Focus on creating Special Candies and activating combinations – this will assist in both fulfilling orders, and clearing the path to the Special Candies at the bottom of the game board.

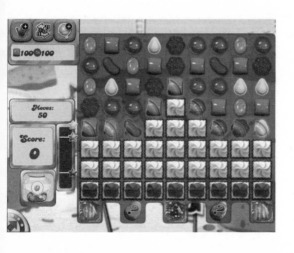

CANDY KINGDOM: Level 377

FOCUS ON

FOCUSING ON clearing the Liquorice, so that you can start work on clearing the Cake Bomb.

WATCH OUT FOR

MAKE SURE not to activate Line Blasts or Wrapped Explosions unless the Cake Bomb is in the blast radius. Don't activate the Colour Bomb with the Candy you need to fulfil orders. Aim to combine with another Candy, and trust that the cascade will result in collecting Candies for your orders.

CANDY KINGDOM: Level 382

FOCUS ON

THE MOST efficient way to clear this level is to create and activate Special Candies to clear those pesky blockers. With the right strategy, and just a sprinkling of luck, aim to activate a Colour Bomb + Colour Bomb Combination.

WATCH OUT FOR

KEEP AN eye on the Chocolate Fountain. It's not going anywhere, so make sure that Chocolate doesn't grow out of control.

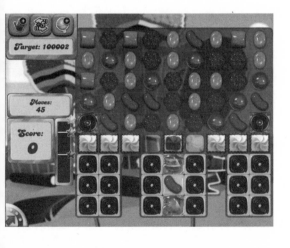

CANDY KINGDOM: Level 391

FOCUS ON

FOR THE first few moves, focus on fulfilling the orders while clearing the Frosting. When the countdown timer on the Candy Bombs is low, activate a Colour Bomb + Colour Bomb combination to clear them in one move.

WATCH OUT FOR

ENSURE YOU'VE don't clear all the Marmalade, and activate the Colour Bombs too early on in the game. You'll need to reserve some Colour Bombs to assist you in fulfilling the orders later in the game.

CANDY KINGDOM: Level 410

FOCUS ON
ENSURE TO remove the clear Jelly surrounding the Chocolate Fountain. Clear the Marmalade so the Striped Candies become available - activate these to clear the Candy Bombs. The winning combination for this level is a Colour Bomb + Striped Candy combination.

WATCH OUT FOR
KEEP AN eye on the Chocolate Fountain. It's not going anywhere, so make sure that Chocolate doesn't grow out of control.

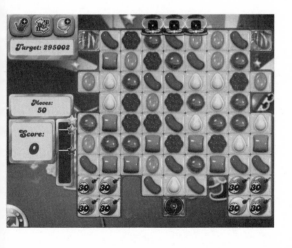

CANDY KINGDOM: Level 434

FOCUS ON

BEFORE YOU tackle the clear Jelly, ridding the game board of the Candy Bombs is a priority.

WATCH OUT FOR

IF POSSIBLE, hold off on clearing the Frosting above the Chocolate Fountain as long as you can. If you utilize this strategy, you'll be blessed with some Chocolate-free time on the game board.

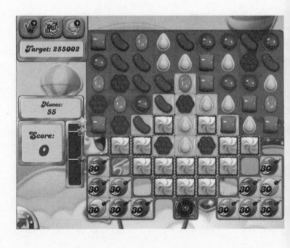

CANDY KINGDOM: Level 445

FOCUS ON

AVOID CLEARING the Frosting on the far sides of the game board. By implementing this strategy, the Ingredients will move down the parallel rows, saving you the trouble of moving and switching them yourself.

WATCH OUT FOR

IF YOU clear Frosting on the far side of the game board, the ingredients are likely to slip back into the wrong row. Avoid this by ensuring you don't clear Frosting if it's next to Ingredients – unless it's in the centre of the game board.

CANDY KINGDOM: Level 452

FOCUS ON — TO FULFIL orders, you'll need some extra special combinations. Make some strategic moves to create a Striped Candy and a Colour Bomb – combine these two, and you'll have your orders fulfilled quickly and efficiently.

WATCH OUT FOR — KEEP AN eye on the Chocolate – it can easily grow out of control. This is where those Special Candies come in handy.

CANDY KINGDOM: Level 461

FOCUS ON

TO FULFIL orders, you'll need some extra special combinations. Make some strategic moves to create a Striped Candy and a Colour Bomb – combine these two, and you'll have your orders fulfilled quickly and efficiently. Hang on to those Swedish Fish for those hard to reach clear Jellies.

WATCH OUT FOR

KEEP AN eye on the Chocolate – it can easily grow out of control. This is where those Special Candies come in handy.

CANDY KINGDOM: Level 480

FOCUS ON
REMOVING THE Liquorice and the clear Jellies lurking beneath it – it's the trickiest part of the level!

WATCH OUT FOR
DON'T BE tempted to clear the Marmalade and activate the Striped Candies too soon – they might end up being your life saver at a later stage.

CANDY KINGDOM: Level 492

FOCUS ON

A DELICIOUS challenge awaits you in the form of hidden clear Jelly, Multi Layered Frosting, a Chocolate Fountain, and all six Candy colours.

To clear this level you'll need to focus on creating Special Candies, and activating combinations such as the Super Line Blast and Double Wrapped Explosion, as well as combining with Colour Bombs. This strategy will open up the board by clearing the Frosting and any Chocolate accumulating at the bottom of the game board.

WATCH OUT FOR

AVOID ACTIVATING the Swedish Fish too early in the game; you'll want to save these for those clear Jellies that are tricky to reach!

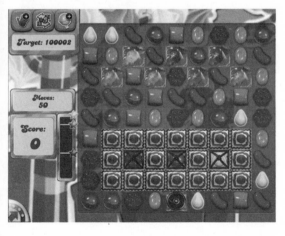

CANDY KINGDOM: Level 500

FOCUS ON

PRIORITIZE CLEARING the Frosting and the Cake Bomb simultaneously. If you plan ahead, save one segment from each of the Cake Bombs, thus creating a chain reaction when one Cake Bomb is cleared.

When the Candy Cannon starts to dispense Ingredients, aim to create vertical Striped Candies, to assist with clearing any leftover Frosting, and bring those Ingredients down quickly and efficiently.

WATCH OUT FOR

AIM TO keep the Liquorice Lock at the top of the game board for as long as possible, so as to avoid the Candy Bombs the Candy Cannon will dispense.

CANDY KINGDOM: Level 530

FOCUS ON

CREATING LINE Blasts and Wrapped Explosions. It's the fastest and most effective way to open up the game board, especially if you can activate a Double Wrapped Explosion.

WATCH OUT FOR

THE FROSTING – leave it be if you can, as it blocks the Chocolate Fountain from creating havoc.

CANDY KINGDOM: Level 534

FOCUS ON

PRIORITIZE CLEARING the Candy Bombs. Once they're clear, focus on creating Special Candies and activating combinations to remove the clear Jelly.

WATCH OUT FOR

DON'T EXHAUST too many moves clearing Frosting, as there are no clear Jellies lurking beneath. If you do clear the Frosting, it should be for the benefit of clearing the game board to make room for combinations and cascades.

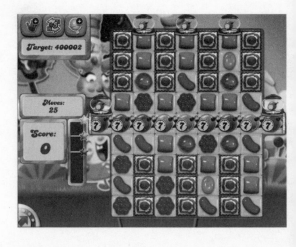

CANDY KINGDOM: Level 565

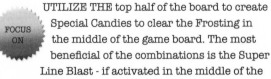

UTILIZE THE top half of the board to create Special Candies to clear the Frosting in the middle of the game board. The most beneficial of the combinations is the Super Line Blast - if activated in the middle of the game board.

Avoid creating matches on the Conveyor Belt; you'll have to worry about the Candy Bombs being dispensed from the Candy Cannons above.

Once the Frosting is cleared, it will open up the game board, thus making it easier to create Colour Bombs. Aim to activate a Colour Bomb with a Wrapped Candy; the result will clear the Frosting efficiently and quickly.

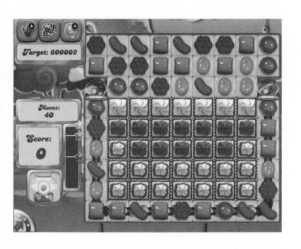

CANDY KINGDOM: 567

FOCUS ON

PRIORITIZE CLEARING the Candy Bombs, followed by the Chocolate and the Liquorice.

After clearing the game board from these blockers, aim to make as many Colour Bomb and Special Candy combinations as possible.

WATCH OUT FOR

KEEP AN eye on the Conveyor Belt – sometimes a little extra luck will come your way, and Candies will align to form a well needed combination.

CANDY KINGDOM: Level 617

FOCUS ON

PRIORITIZE CLEARING the Frosting from the top half of the game board.

Prioritize making strategic moves and matches to create Special Candies. By activating a Line Blast or Wrapped Explosion combination, the task of removing clear Jelly from the corners of the game board will be made easier.

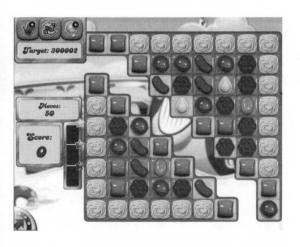

CANDY KINGDOM: Level 740

FOCUS ON UNLOCKING THOSE Sugar Chests – there's clear Jelly hiding underneath, so they'll need extra attention.

When activating a Colour Bomb and Striped Candy combination; if a Sugar Key is changed to a Striped Candy, the Key will activate, and open one layer of the Sugar Chest – awesome!

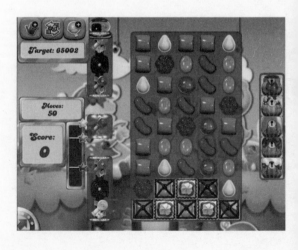

CANDY KINGDOM: Level 827

FOCUS ON

CLEAR THE game board by clearing the Frosting and Multi Level Frosting. This will allow more room to create Special Candies, and activate their combinations. Keep one eye on the Candy Bombs being dispensed from the Candy Cannons, and the other on collecting Sugar Keys.

Save as many Special Candies as you can to make Line Blasts and Wrapped Explosions. If you activate a Colour Bomb with a Striped Candy, ensure its Candy equivalent is also located on that tricky bottom row.

WATCH OUT FOR

CANDY CANNONS are dispensing Candy Bombs at an alarming rate, and the hard-to-reach Clear Jelly is locked away in a Sugar Chest – a challenging level!

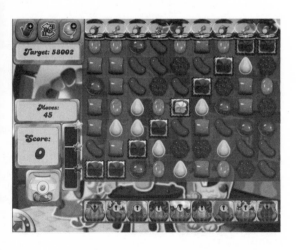

CANDY KINGDOM: Level 844

FOCUS ON

CREATE SPECIAL Candies to the side of the game board, as opposed to the top.

Activating Line Blast and Wrapped Explosion combinations from the side of the game board will make it easier to clear both of the Popcorn at once. If you activate from above or below the Popcorn; one will block the other from being cleared.

Aim to create Special Candies in close proximity to one another. Don't exhaust moves attempting to move them closer together. It is more beneficial to activate them on their own, which will assist in clearing the Frosting.

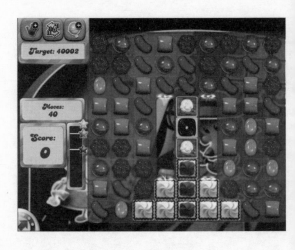

CANDY KINGDOM: Level 875

FOCUS ON PRIORITIZE UNLOCKING the Sugar Chests and opening up access to those Special Candies and Colour Bombs. Once available, make strategic matches to move them down the game board into the path of the Conveyor Belt. You can then activate them when the time is right, and clear that Popcorn.

WATCH OUT FOR ACTIVATING THE Colour Bombs too soon. You may need them later to clear the Chocolate spawned from the Chocolate Fountain, and those rogue clear Jellies.

CANDY KINGDOM: Level 957

FOCUS ON

PRIORITIZE CLEARING the Marmalade on the left-hand side of the game board. This will open up the access to the Teleporter, and provide more space to create combinations and cascades.

WATCH OUT FOR

ALL CLEAR Jellies are located beneath blockers, so make sure you are using your moves strategically to clear those blockers quickly.

CANDY KINGDOM: Level 960

FOCUS ON

IT'S SO tempting to clear the Liquorice Locks first, since their presence is overwhelming, but instead try to clear the Marmalade first. This will open up half the game the board quickly - creating more opportunities for cascades and creation of Special Candies.

Keep your eyes peeled for opportunities to create Special Candies and activate a Double Wrapped Explosion combination. This combination will clear those Liquorice Locks and with some luck, collect more than one Sugar Key. Collect these Sugar Keys as quickly as possible, so you can unlock the Sugar Chest and reveal the clear Jelly.

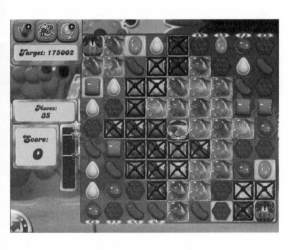

CANDY KINGDOM: Level 1001

Congratulations on making it past Level 1000 –
what a sweet achievement!

 PRIORITIZE UNLOCKING the Sugar Chest.
For every Candy Key collected, a new one
will be dispensed; so collect them as fast
as possible.

While collecting Candy Keys, keep an eye
out for opportunities to create Striped Candies
which will help you clear the Frosting and Liquorice
Locks at the bottom of the game board.

When the Sugar Chest is open and ingredients
are dispensed, make matches that result in the
Ingredients moving to the side of the game board.
This way you won't have to clear the Frosting
underneath the Candy Cannon.

CANDY KINGDOM: Level 1032

PRIORITIZE CLEARING the Marmalade, and opening up the Coconut Liquorice. It's essential in clearing the level.

YOU'VE ONLY got 20 moves for the level, so strategize and re-think every move. Make every move count.

CANDY KINGDOM: Level 1061

FOCUS ON

ACTIVATING LINE Blast and Wrapped Explosions. It's the fastest and most effective way to open up the game board.

WATCH OUT FOR

WHEN CLEARING Liquorice Locks from the Chocolate, don't remove too many at the same time as the Chocolate can easily grow out of control.

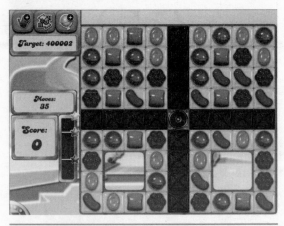

Thank You!

The Candy Crush Saga team is smaller than many people probably think, and we are truly thankful and amazed that we have so many dedicated players. It's more than anyone imagined when the game was first released back in 2012.

We could put a long list of personal thank you's here - so many family members, friends, pets, old teachers and mentors - all individuals who we can thank for being where we are today. However, we would not be where we are if it weren't for YOU - cheesy as that may sound.

So, to all of our players, anywhere from level 1 up to infinity - Thank You!